GEORGE WASHINGTON

BY CHERYL HARNESS

■ NATIONAL GEOGRAPHIC SOCIETY

WASHINGTON, D.C.

Towns, lakes, counties, a state, our nation's capital and the tallest monument in it are named after him. He's a man of myths—of wooden teeth and a chopped-down cherry tree. We see his face in cold white marble, on the money in our pockets, on the walls of schoolrooms, and in advertisements every February. We see a legendary hero so often that we don't see the uncertain man whose belief in liberty drove him to conquer his doubts—and an empire. He might have been just a rich farmer in one of the 13 colonies of British America, but that wasn't his whole story. Not by a long shot.

Until the Revolutionary War was fought and a nation was born, few knew how remarkable he really was.

Not even George Washington himself.

George Washington was born in 1732. He grew up tall and sturdy, playing and working with his little sister and brothers and the children of the black slaves who lived on his father's farms. Kind, easygoing Gus Washington expected to send his son George to his old school in England. But Gus died when George was only 11 years old.

So George hunted, fished, and copied out his lessons in his home colony of Virginia. He rode horses—the faster the better—and dreamed of adventure. He set his heart on a military career. He'd wear the red coat of a British officer, as had his older, much admired half brother Lawrence. Maybe one day George would command a royal warship. But would his strict mother, Mary, let him go to sea? No.

She was definite about that.

George was mad and disappointed. He was definite about that! How could he know that he'd already made a discovery that would lead him to amazing adventures beyond his very best daydreams?

The ancient art of *Surveying or Measuring Land* began in EGYPT. It is based on geometry. Surveyors use a small telescope (a transit) on a tripod, a compass, chains, and other tools to find land boundaries and positions.

some of George's surveying travels

0   50   100 miles

When George was 13 years old, he had found his grandfather's surveying tools. Within three years, George was part of a surveying expedition in the Virginia frontier, hacking through forests; swimming his horse across fast, rushing rivers; and watching Indians dance by firelight.

By age 17, George was a professional surveyor, a tough, athletic frontiersman. He saved his pay to buy land. He took fencing lessons and devoured books so he'd be quick with a sword and quick with his mind. He spent more and more time with his wealthy neighbors, the Fairfaxes of Belvoir (tall, shy George had a crush on Sally Fairfax), and at Lawrence's farm, Mount Vernon. George loved his brilliant but frail half brother, and there were dances to be danced, clever talk to be listened to—and a bossy mother to be avoided.

George was determined to be somebody and make his own way in the world.

The King of England wanted men to keep the forests north and west of Virginia under his control and out of the hands of his archenemy, the King of France. Twenty-one-year-old George, a skilled woodsman, saw his chance to fulfill his boyhood dreams of military glory. He presented himself to the colonial governor at Williamsburg and became an officer in the Virginia militia. He'd read books about military strategy, but his true education was fighting alongside British soldiers.

THE FRENCH and INDIAN WAR

was the last conflict between FRANCE, GREAT BRITAIN, and their INDIAN allies for control of NORTH AMERICA. When the peace treaty was signed in 1763, BRITAIN had won control of the territory east of the MISSISSIPPI RIVER.

MISSISSIPPI RIVER

QUEBEC

FORT TICONDEROGA

FORT DUQUESNE
FORT NECESSITY

OHIO RIVER

☐ BRITISH
☐ FRENCH
☐ SPANISH

LAND CLAIMS

He saw them paraded through the woods in their bright red coats, just asking to be ambushed! George nearly drowned, starved, froze, and almost died of fever in the forests. He heard the whistle of bullets tearing through his jacket and the screams of horses shot out from under him; smelled the hot blood and smoke. He saw (and remembered) that British generals, too proud to listen to a colonial soldier, could be beaten.

Years of hardship and illness on the frontier had left Colonel Washington worn and weary. He'd met a young lady, Martha Custis, whom he liked very much. Her wealthy husband had died and left her with a little boy and girl. George liked them, too. He decided to get married, hang up his uniform, and settle down at Mount Vernon, left to him by his much admired Lawrence, who had died.

For the next 16 years, George Washington was a hardworking and prosperous experimental farmer. He loved his family and his land, his books, and hunting foxes with his horses and hounds.

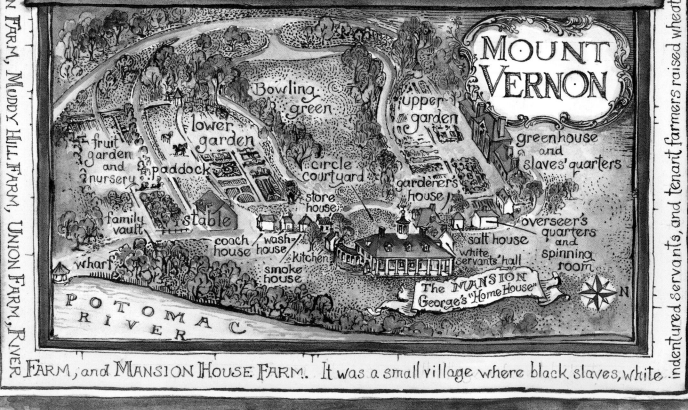

MOUNT VERNON

Bowling green

lower garden

upper garden

greenhouse and slaves' quarters

fruit garden and nursery

paddock

circle courtyard

gardener's house

store house

family vault

stable

coach house

wash-house

kitchen

smoke house

salt house

white servants' hall

overseer's quarters and spinning room

wharf

The MANSION George's "Home House"

N

POTOMAC RIVER

MOUNT VERNON was made up of five small farms: DOGUE RUN FARM, MUDDY HILL FARM, UNION FARM, RIVER FARM, and MANSION HOUSE FARM. It was a small village where black slaves, white indentured servants, and tenant farmers raised wheat, corn, flax, tobacco, sheep, horses, cattle, and pigs. They fished, spun, cooked, wove cloth, made bricks, and milled flour.

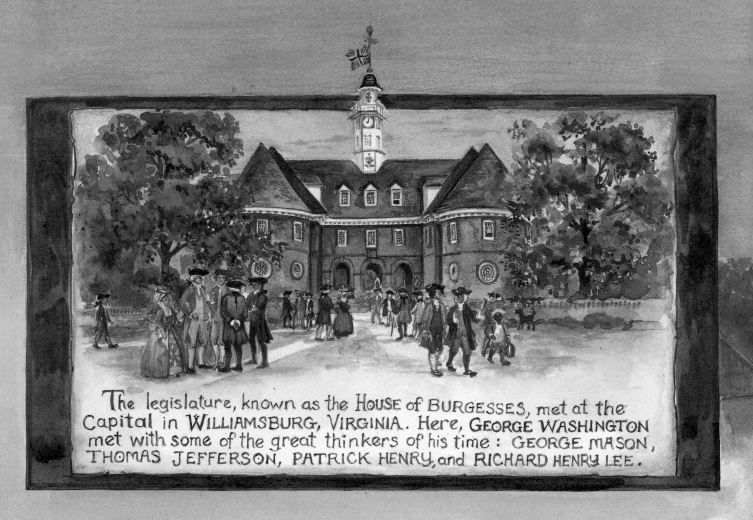

The legislature, known as the HOUSE of BURGESSES, met at the Capital in WILLIAMSBURG, VIRGINIA. Here, GEORGE WASHINGTON met with some of the great thinkers of his time: GEORGE MASON, THOMAS JEFFERSON, PATRICK HENRY, and RICHARD HENRY LEE.

His neighbors elected George to the legislature at Williamsburg, where the political talk was getting hotter. King George III and his subjects in America weren't getting along very well.

George Washington complained about "our lordly Masters" over in London making tax laws without any say-so from America. When the King slapped a tax on tea, George angrily switched to coffee.

Colonists in Massachusetts protested even more dramatically: *Splash!* went the tea into Boston Harbor on a cold December night in 1773. In response, the furious King closed the port. No ships in—no ships out. This was serious.

Throughout the Colonies, folks were upset about the situation: What happened to one could happen to all 13. They began writing to each other—not as Virginians or York Staters or Georgians, but as Americans. This was new.

In the late summer of 1774, George gathered with 55 other colonial representatives at a Continental Congress in Philadelphia, Pennsylvania. There it was decided that none of the Colonies would trade with their mother country until the King was persuaded to treat them fairly, as loyal British citizens. The men pledged to meet again in the spring, but by then the long battle of words with Britain had turned into a battle of bullets in the villages of Lexington and Concord, Massachusetts. This was war!

George Washington
VIRGINIA

Samuel Adams,
MASSACHUSETTS

Josiah Bartlett
NEW HAMPSHIRE

George Walton
GEORGIA

William Paca
MARYLAND

George Read
DELAWARE

William Hooper
NORTH CAROLINA

John Adams
MASSACHUSETTS

William Ellery
RHODE ISLAND

Robert Livingston
NEW YORK

The colonists knew they were going to need an army and a general to lead it. Who had military experience? Who was rich and important enough to show the King they were serious?

Tall, calm-looking, 43-year-old George stood up slowly, bowed to the other delegates at the Second Continental Congress, and thanked them for choosing him. He wasn't at all sure he could do the job, but he said softly, "I will enter upon the momentous duty and exert every power I possess for the support of the glorious cause."

What if he failed? He and his country would be ruined. They all knew it. Thomas Jefferson, Benjamin Franklin, John Adams, John Hancock, and absolutely General George Washington would all be arrested, taken to England in chains, and executed. That's what happened to traitors.

MASSACHUSETTS

SOUTH CAROLINA

CONNECTICUT

VIRGINIA

NEW HAMPSHIRE

PENNSYLVANIA

PENNSYLVANIA

LAKE ERIE

George began puzzling out what he had to do even before
he went to Massachusetts to meet the soldiers gathered
there: 16,000 men worried about their families back home
and not used to being bossed around. They had hardly
any guns, powder, or cannon. George and his officers
knew they must discipline and unite these men and
lead them in battle against the army and navy
of the most powerful empire on Earth.

PROCLAMATION LINE OF 1763

MARYLAND

Potomac River

The Earl of
Dunmore, the last
Royal Governor of
VIRGINIA
gathers an army.
It is defeated by the
patriots,
December 9,
1775

James River

Williamsburg

NORTH
CAROLINA

SOUTH
CAROLINA

GEORGIA

Savannah River

Pee Dee River

June 28, 1776

British
warships
fire on
Charleston

February 27, 1776
1,500 Scottish Tories
are defeated by
1,000 patriots
at Moores Creek
Bridge

Wilmington

Savannah

ATLANTIC OCEAN

0   50   100 miles

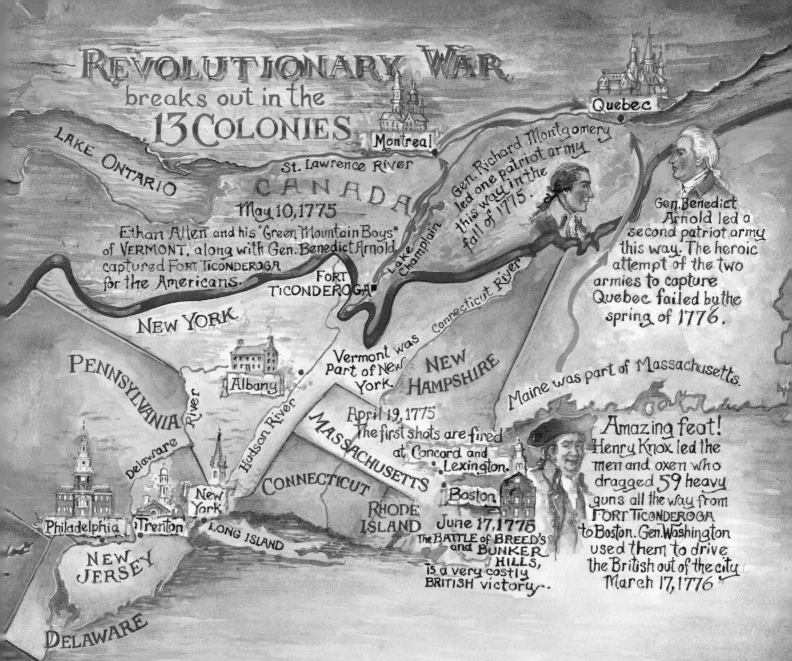

REVOLUTIONARY WAR
breaks out in the
13 COLONIES

Quebec

Montreal

LAKE ONTARIO

St. Lawrence River

CANADA

May 10, 1775

Ethan Allen and his "Green Mountain Boys" of VERMONT, along with Gen. Benedict Arnold, captured FORT TICONDEROGA for the Americans.

Gen. Richard Montgomery led one patriot army this way in the fall of 1775.

Gen. Benedict Arnold led a second patriot army this way. The heroic attempt of the two armies to capture Quebec failed by the spring of 1776.

NEW YORK

FORT TICONDEROGA

Lake Champlain

Connecticut River

Vermont was part of New York.

NEW HAMPSHIRE

Maine was part of Massachusetts.

PENNSYLVANIA

Albany

Hudson River

Delaware River

MASSACHUSETTS

April 19, 1775
The first shots are fired at Concord and Lexington.

CONNECTICUT

New York

RHODE ISLAND

Boston

Amazing feat! Henry Knox led the men and oxen who dragged 59 heavy guns all the way from FORT TICONDEROGA to Boston. Gen. Washington used them to drive the British out of the city March 17, 1776

Philadelphia

Trenton

LONG ISLAND

June 17, 1775
The BATTLE of BREED'S and BUNKER HILLS, is a very costly BRITISH victory.

NEW JERSEY

DELAWARE

A tense year went by in which George drove the redcoats out of Boston. The Americans tried to capture Canada, but this was a heroic failure. Patriots in the South drove the British governor out of Virginia. Furious, George III smashed down his fist. He'd shut down all American ports. He'd hire extra soldiers: the feared Hessians of Germany. He'd crush this rebellion!

People were choosing up sides. At least a third of the Americans were Tories. They wanted to stay with Britain. They either fled or fought against their neighbors: civil war! Native Americans mostly sided with the British against the Americans, who were taking more and more of their lands: Indian war! France was Britain's sworn enemy. Perhaps she would help the patriots: world war!

O! ye that love mankind! Ye that dare oppose not only the tyranny but the tyrant, stand forth!
—Thomas Paine

We hold these Truths to be self-evident, that all Men are created equal, that they are endowed by their Creator with certain unalienable Rights, that among these are Life, Liberty, and the Pursuit of Happiness~

The Americans' blood was up: Rights as British citizens? Bah! Now was the time for boldness! A chance to change the world forever! Break away! They'd make their own country where people governed themselves. THAT was the American Revolution.

On July 4, 1776, the delegates at the Continental Congress in Philadelphia pledged to each other "their Lives, their Fortunes, and their Sacred Honour" and signed the solemn Declaration of Independence, but George Washington wasn't there to add his name. He was in New York getting ready for the battle of his—and his country's—life.

Patriots in New York City melted down the big statue of King George III on a Horse into 42,088 bullets, but no statue was big enough for all the bullets they were going to need.

A huge fleet of British warships—the biggest
ever—was sailing into New York harbor. Their masts
looked like a forest of trees clouded with white sails. They
carried more than 34,000 British and Hessian warriors. The
sun glinted sparks off their helmets and bayonets. The Spirit
of '76 turned to terror.

On a clear August morning, George sat tall and straight
in his saddle. His blue eyes burned into those of his men as
he said, "If I see any man turn his back today, I will shoot
him through. I have two pistols loaded, but I will not ask
any man to go farther than I do. I will fight so long as I have
a leg or an arm."

The patriots fought, fled, and bravely fought some more against the King's soldiers, stabbing at them with 21-inch-long bayonets. The Americans would have been trapped on the shores of Long Island and the war lost that very summer of 1776 if their grim, steady general hadn't led the thousands of men, guns, oxen, and horses away from capture in a huge, daring foggy-night retreat to Manhattan Island across the wide East River.

When hordes of redcoats in full battle cry, smoke, and thunder attacked them on the 15th of September, the Americans panicked and ran. George shouted after his men. He slashed the air with his saber in a purple fury. New York City was lost and burning—but once again, the patriots narrowly escaped.

George mastered his temper and rallied his troops to fight again and again. As summer turned to fall, the British chased him and his rebel army like a fox up though the villages, woods, and fields of Manhattan and New Jersey. Then the British commander decided to settle his soldiers into winter quarters and wrap things up in the spring. It was getting too cold for fighting.

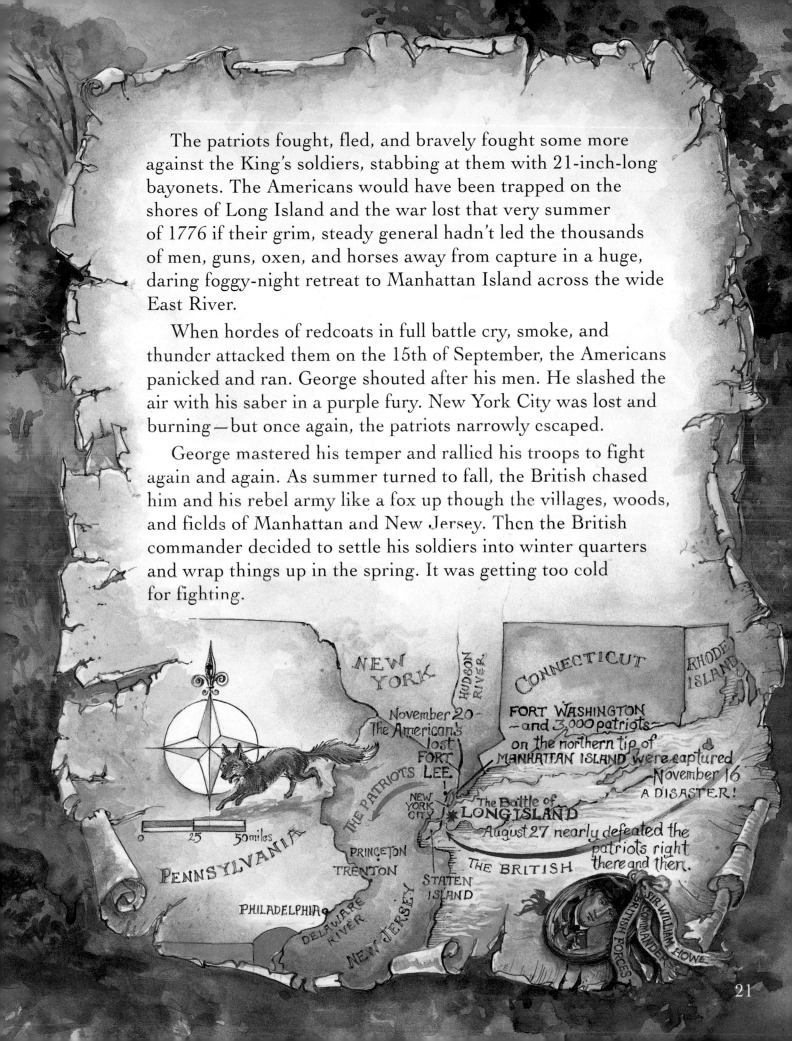

NEW YORK

HUDSON RIVER

CONNECTICUT

RHODE ISLAND

November 20 — The Americans lost FORT LEE.

FORT WASHINGTON —and 3,000 patriots— on the northern tip of MANHATTAN ISLAND were captured November 16 A DISASTER!

THE PATRIOTS

NEW YORK CITY

The Battle of LONG ISLAND August 27 nearly defeated the patriots right there and then.

THE BRITISH

PENNSYLVANIA

0 25 50 miles

PRINCETON
TRENTON

STATEN ISLAND

PHILADELPHIA

DELAWARE RIVER

NEW JERSEY

SIR WILLIAM HOWE BRITISH COMMANDER BRITISH FORCES

The shivering, hungry Americans muttered around their campfires. They'd only signed up until the end of 1776— just a few days more, then, by God, they'd go home to their families, who needed them. Their general begged the powerless Congress for supplies for his men and got little or nothing.

George the fox had to outlast the hunter. He'd get money for his men if he had to pay them out of his own pocket. What could he say to beg them to stay? One of his soldiers, Thomas Paine, wrote just the right words.

These are the times that try men's souls. The summer soldier and the sunshine patriot will, in this crisis, shrink from the service of their country; but he that stands it now, deserves the love and thanks of man and woman. Tyranny, like hell, is not easily conquered; yet we have this consolation with us, that the harder the conflict, the more glorious the triumph.

But George needed more than words. He needed
a victory, and he needed it now. He'd surprise-attack
the Hessian soldiers across the river. The tall, calm
Virginian would make his soldiers see that this was
"Victory or Death" for the American Revolution.

George and his officers led more than 2,500 freezing, starving, sleepy men plus their animals to the banks of the icy Delaware River. They crossed over, then slipped and stumbled all that black, bitter Christmas night for nine miles on numb feet, bleeding in the snow. They beat the Hessians and captured the town of Trenton in the morning.

George, who hadn't slept in four days, flashed a rare smile and said, "...this is a glorious day for our country."

A week later the exhausted patriots won another battle at Princeton when George fooled the British into thinking the Americans were where they weren't. There was hope. George had kept the Revolution alive to fight another day.

Valley Forge

After being defeated at Germantown and Brandywine, Pennsylvania, George and his army of 11,000 men spent the winter of 1777~78 at VALLEY FORGE. More than 3,000 men died there of cold, hunger, and sickness. What kept them going? George Washington's leadership, Baron von Steuben's training, and the news that General Burgoyne's redcoats had been licked at SARATOGA. Now FRANCE openly joined the war against GREAT BRITAIN. "No news was received with more heartfelt joy," said George. This was the turning point of the REVOLUTIONARY WAR.

PENNSYLVANIA

PRINCETON, N.J. Jan. 3, 1777

TRENTON, N.J. Dec. 26, 1776

VALLEY FORGE

PHILADELPHIA Sept. 26, 1777

BRANDYWINE Sept. 11, 1777

MARYLAND

NEW JERSEY

DELAWARE

OUT WEST, Colonel George Rogers Clark and his "Kentucky Long Knives" fought a heroic but brutal war against the BRITISH and their INDIAN allies in what is now ILLINOIS and INDIANA.

BARON VON STEUBEN

MARQUIS DE LAFAYETTE

VIRGINIA

Oct. 19, 1781 YORKTOWN

"We fight, get beat, rise, and fight again." General Nathanael Greene, commander of American forces in the SOUTH

a draw at GUILFORD COURT HOUSE, Mar. 15, 1781

NORTH CAROLINA

COWPENS Jan. 17, 1781

KINGS MOUNTAIN Oct. 7, 1780

CORNWALLIS

CLINTON

Big battles went on as well as a truly ugly war of terror between TORY and PATRIOT civilians.

CAMDEN Aug. 16, 1780

SOUTH CAROLINA

GEORGIA

CHARLESTON May 12, 1780

COMTE DE ROCHAMBEAU commander of FRENCH forces

The British commander, cautious Sir Henry Clinton, expected an attack at New York, but George went south to Yorktown, Virginia, trapping General Charles, Lord Cornwallis between a combined army of French and patriot soldiers and a fleet of French ships.
Cornwallis was forced to surrender on the 19th of October, 1781 ~ but he was far too proud to personally give up his sword to General George Washington.

SAVANNAH Dec. 29, 1778

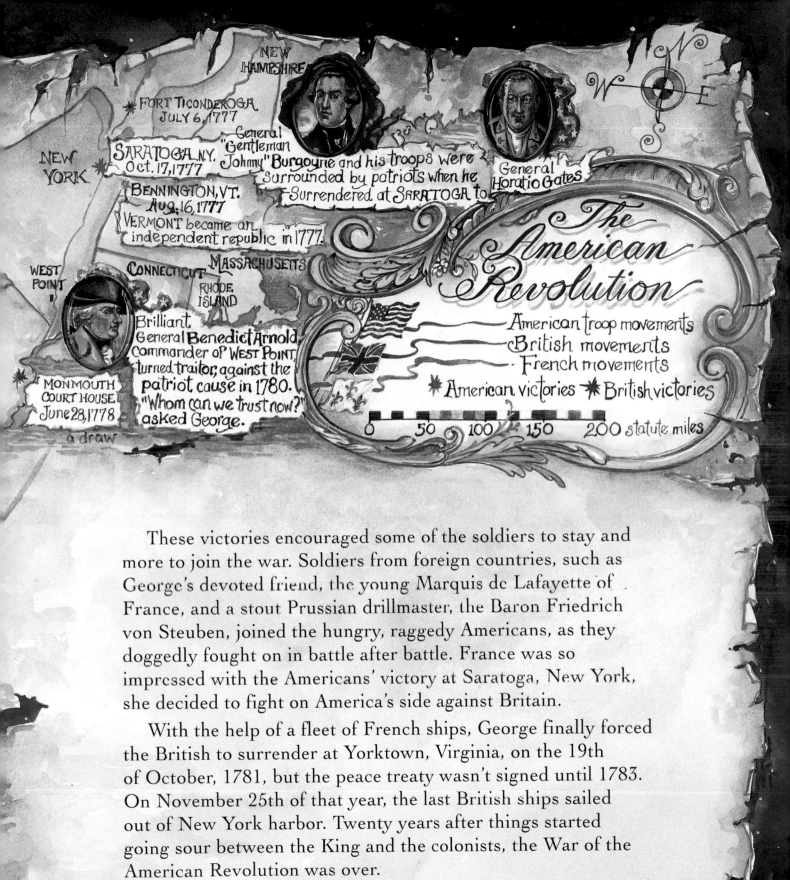

The American Revolution

NEW HAMPSHIRE

FORT TICONDEROGA
JULY 6, 1777

General "Gentleman Johnny" Burgoyne and his troops were surrounded by patriots when he surrendered at SARATOGA to

General Horatio Gates

NEW YORK

SARATOGA, N.Y.
Oct. 17, 1777

BENNINGTON, VT.
Aug. 16, 1777
VERMONT became an independent republic in 1777.

MASSACHUSETTS

WEST POINT

CONNECTICUT
RHODE ISLAND

Brilliant General Benedict Arnold, commander of WEST POINT, turned traitor against the patriot cause in 1780. "Whom can we trust now?" asked George.

MONMOUTH COURT HOUSE
June 28, 1778
a draw

American troop movements
British movements
French movements
★ American victories ★ British victories

0   50   100   150   200 statute miles

These victories encouraged some of the soldiers to stay and more to join the war. Soldiers from foreign countries, such as George's devoted friend, the young Marquis de Lafayette of France, and a stout Prussian drillmaster, the Baron Friedrich von Steuben, joined the hungry, raggedy Americans, as they doggedly fought on in battle after battle. France was so impressed with the Americans' victory at Saratoga, New York, she decided to fight on America's side against Britain.

With the help of a fleet of French ships, George finally forced the British to surrender at Yorktown, Virginia, on the 19th of October, 1781, but the peace treaty wasn't signed until 1783. On November 25th of that year, the last British ships sailed out of New York harbor. Twenty years after things started going sour between the King and the colonists, the War of the American Revolution was over.

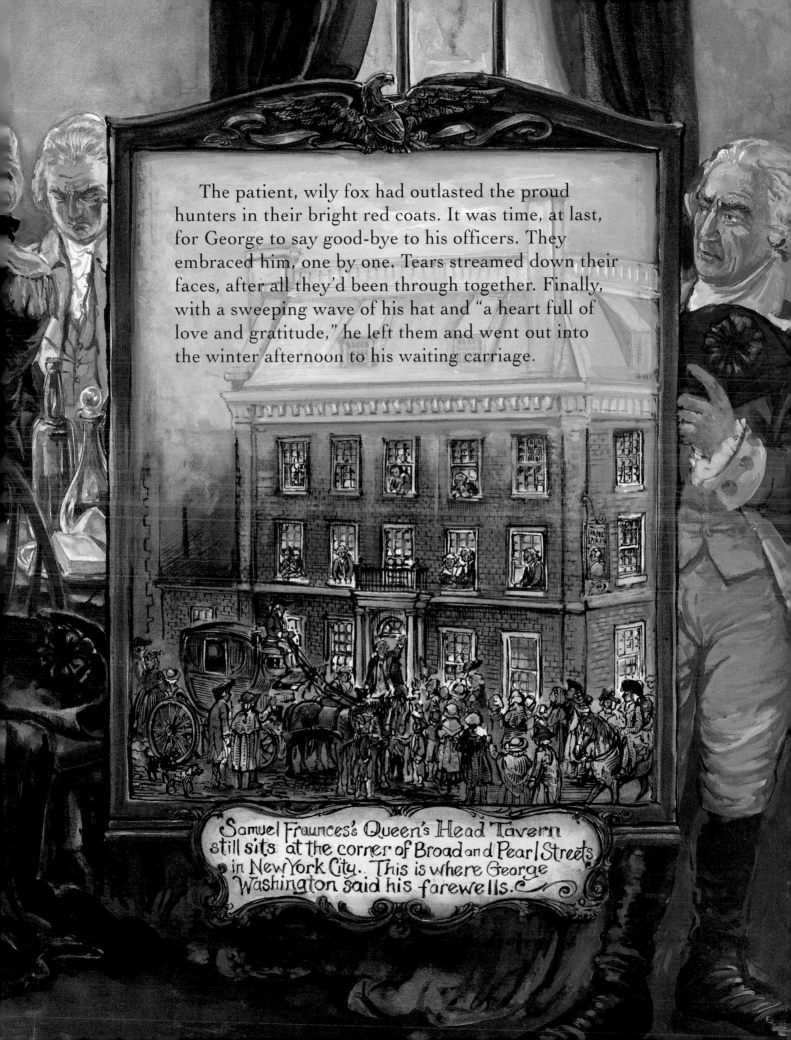

The patient, wily fox had outlasted the proud hunters in their bright red coats. It was time, at last, for George to say good-bye to his officers. They embraced him, one by one. Tears streamed down their faces, after all they'd been through together. Finally, with a sweeping wave of his hat and "a heart full of love and gratitude," he left them and went out into the winter afternoon to his waiting carriage.

Samuel Fraunces's Queen's Head Tavern still sits at the corner of Broad and Pearl Streets in New York City. This is where George Washington said his farewells.

In Annapolis, Maryland, where the Continental Congress was currently meeting, General George Washington did something truly revolutionary: He resigned as commander in chief of the army on December 19, 1783. This was a bolt of lightning for people on both sides of the Atlantic Ocean.

His countrymen loved him. With his stubborn confidence in America's liberty, it was as if George Washington was the Revolution. He had an army that trusted him. Why not use it to seize power and rule as King of the United States? But he was walking away from power? Just like that? Even King George III said that if the general could give up a throne, he'd be the greatest man of the whole 18th century. George could and did and was.

Now, his voice and hands trembling, George stood before the Congress and said farewell. He'd done his job. He knew his country would "stand or fall" depending on how her people governed themselves. Only that would show, George knew, whether the Revolution was a "blessing or a curse" for the present age and for the "unborn millions."

George was a tired old soldier when he finally returned to Mount Vernon. He got home in time for Christmas.

Over the next four years, George and plenty of other Americans saw that their country needed a stronger central government to keep peace at home and gain respect abroad. It needed to pay the nation's debts and regulate trade between 13 stiff-necked, independent states.

In Philadelphia once more, in the humid summer of 1787, 55 hot, flustered men argued out a beautifully strong yet flexible United States Constitution: a set of laws by which people could govern themselves. It wasn't perfect, but it seemed to George, who patiently presided over the Constitutional Convention, "little short of a miracle."

The federal government would have the legislative branch, headed by the Congress, to make the laws; the judicial branch, headed by the Supreme Court, to explain the laws; and the executive branch, headed by a president, to enforce them. It didn't take much arguing to decide who that should be.

A key identifying the people in this painting appears on page 48.

We, the People of the United States, in Order to form a more perfect Union, establish Justice, insure domestic Tranquility, provide for the common defense, promote the general Welfare, and secure the Blessings of Liberty to ourselves and our Posterity, do ordain and establish this Constitution for the United States of America.

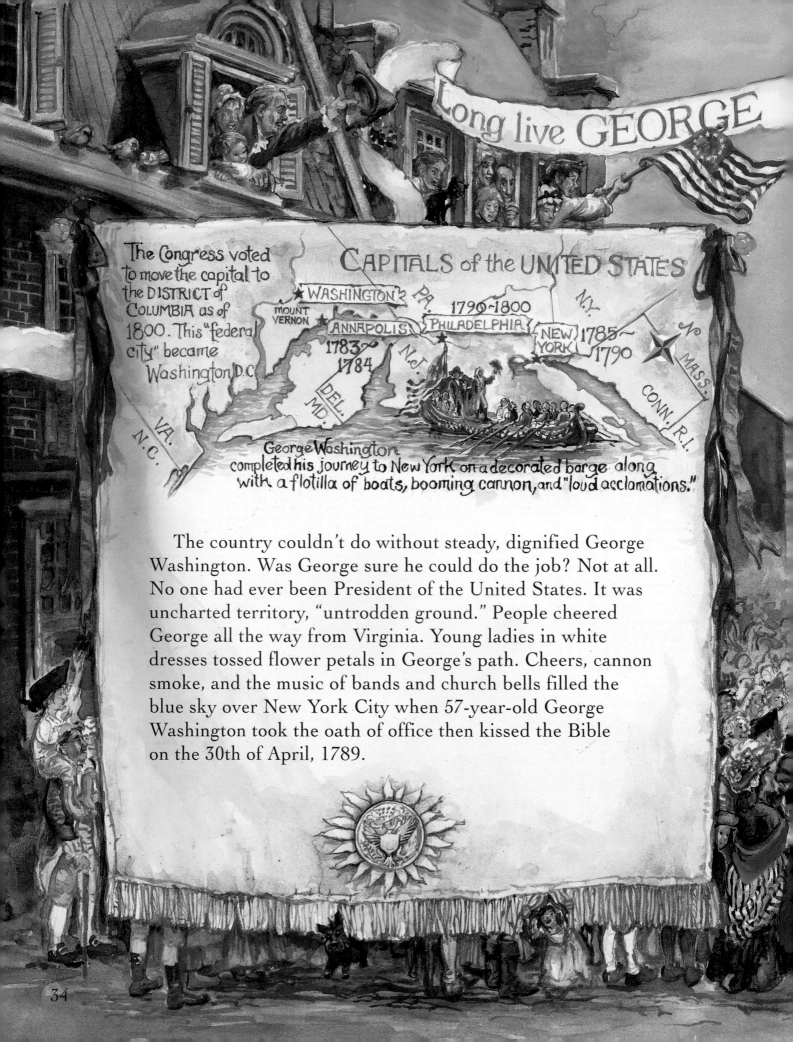

Long live GEORGE

CAPITALS of the UNITED STATES

The Congress voted to move the capital to the DISTRICT of COLUMBIA as of 1800. This "federal city" became Washington D.C.

WASHINGTON
MOUNT VERNON
ANNAPOLIS 1783~ 1784
PA. 1790~1800
PHILADELPHIA
N.Y.
NEW YORK 1785~ 1790
N.J.
DEL.
MD.
VA.
N.C.
MASS.
CONN. R.I.

George Washington completed his journey to New York on a decorated barge along with a flotilla of boats, booming cannon, and "loud acclamations."

The country couldn't do without steady, dignified George Washington. Was George sure he could do the job? Not at all. No one had ever been President of the United States. It was uncharted territory, "untrodden ground." People cheered George all the way from Virginia. Young ladies in white dresses tossed flower petals in George's path. Cheers, cannon smoke, and the music of bands and church bells filled the blue sky over New York City when 57-year-old George Washington took the oath of office then kissed the Bible on the 30th of April, 1789.

WASHINGTON

President

of

the

United States of America!

He served two terms in office, from 1789 to 1797. George and
Martha had to design their roles. Everything they did would be
setting the pattern for how things would be done in the unimaginable
future. Would George be called His Highness? How about
His Exalted High Mightiness? George decided on Mister President.
Martha was called Lady Washington, then First Lady.

Citizens craned their necks to see their war-hero President in
the cream-colored carriage of state drawn by six milk-white horses.

He went on trips to see how the country was doing from New England to the South. Mainly, he was determined that he and his nation should behave and be treated with dignity and respect.

George spent a lot of time with architects designing the new Federal City being built on land bought from Virginia and Maryland. In the summer of 1791, he chose the spot where the President's House still stands. The government, Congress decided, would move to what would become Washington, D.C., before the end of 1800.

It took all of George's fairness and patience to tackle his biggest problem, an argument that divided his Cabinet (his advisers) and the nation. It still goes on today: How strong should the national government be? People who were for a powerful central government, such as Alexander Hamilton, were called Federalists. People who were for less government at the top and stronger rights for the states and the people, such as Thomas Jefferson, were called Democratic-Republicans. Although he tended toward Federalist ideas, George hated political parties and the bitter conflicts they caused between his friends.

The Democratic-Republicans also favored American support of revolutionary France in her war with Britain. Hadn't France sided with America? But the revolution in France had turned into a Reign of Terror. French aristocrats, such as the Marquis de Lafayette, were being thrown into prison. The King and Queen had their heads cut off.

Alexander Hamilton, Secretary of the Treasury

George Washington, President

Henry Knox, Secretary of War

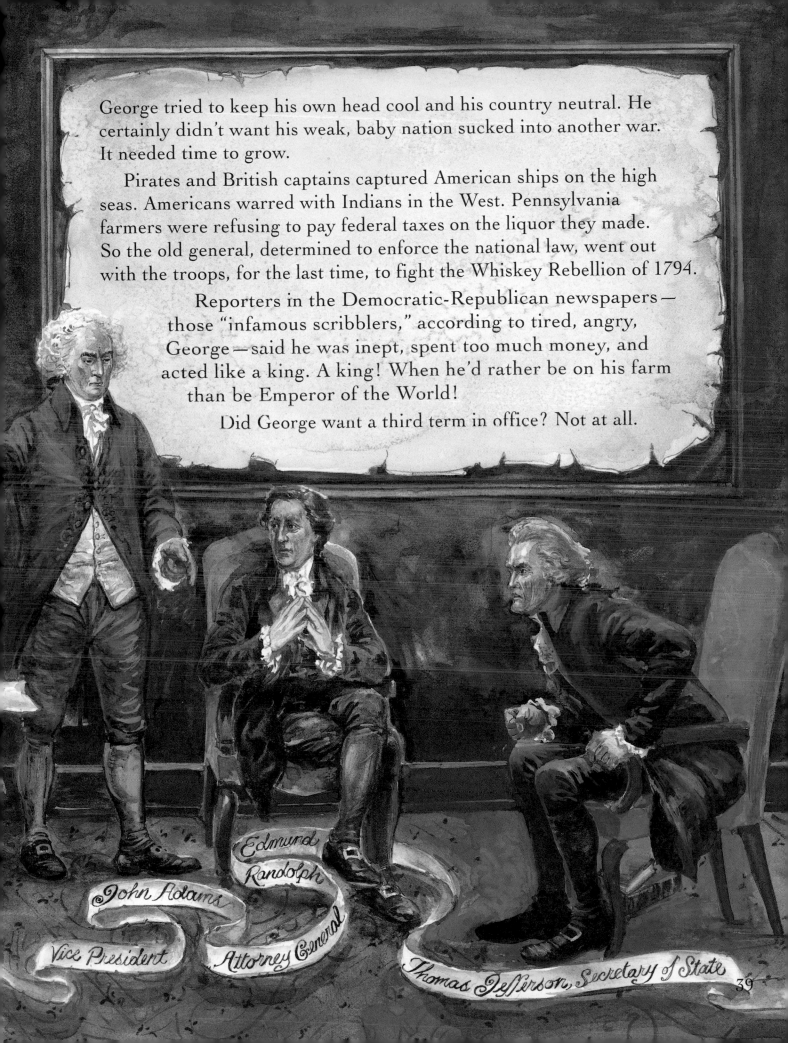

George tried to keep his own head cool and his country neutral. He certainly didn't want his weak, baby nation sucked into another war. It needed time to grow.

Pirates and British captains captured American ships on the high seas. Americans warred with Indians in the West. Pennsylvania farmers were refusing to pay federal taxes on the liquor they made. So the old general, determined to enforce the national law, went out with the troops, for the last time, to fight the Whiskey Rebellion of 1794.

Reporters in the Democratic-Republican newspapers—those "infamous scribblers," according to tired, angry, George—said he was inept, spent too much money, and acted like a king. A king! When he'd rather be on his farm than be Emperor of the World!

Did George want a third term in office? Not at all.

John Adams
Vice President

Edmund Randolph
Attorney General

Thomas Jefferson, Secretary of State

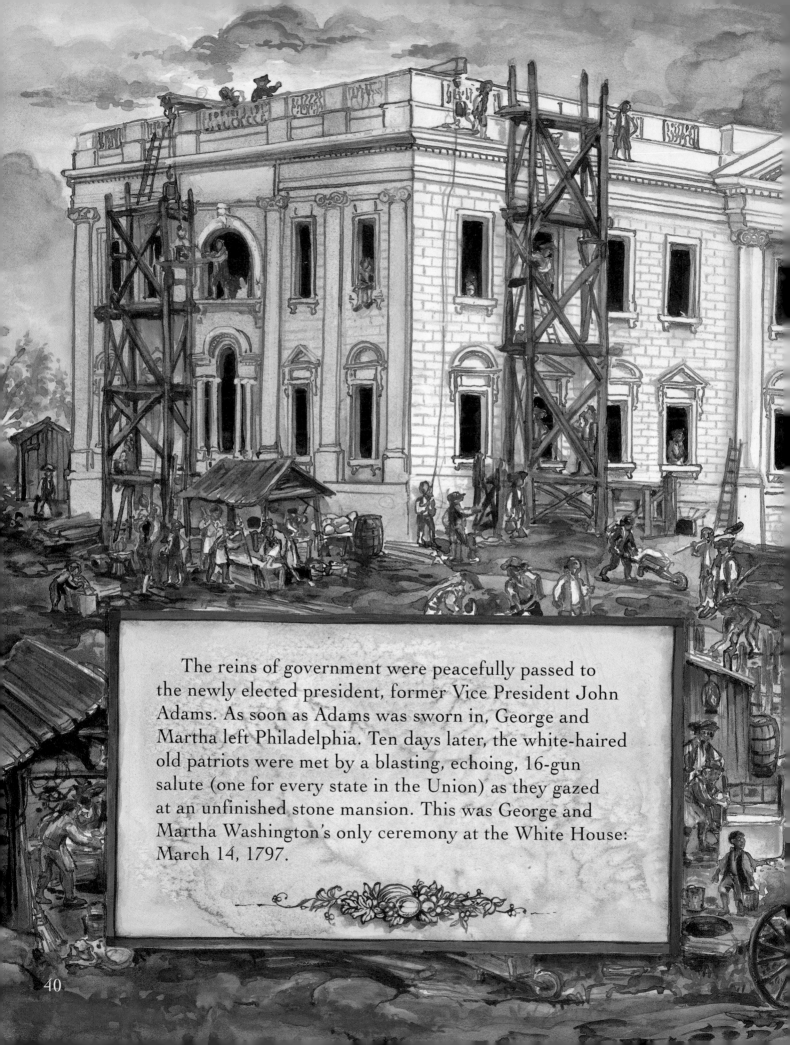

The reins of government were peacefully passed to
the newly elected president, former Vice President John
Adams. As soon as Adams was sworn in, George and
Martha left Philadelphia. Ten days later, the white-haired
old patriots were met by a blasting, echoing, 16-gun
salute (one for every state in the Union) as they gazed
at an unfinished stone mansion. This was George and
Martha Washington's only ceremony at the White House:
March 14, 1797.

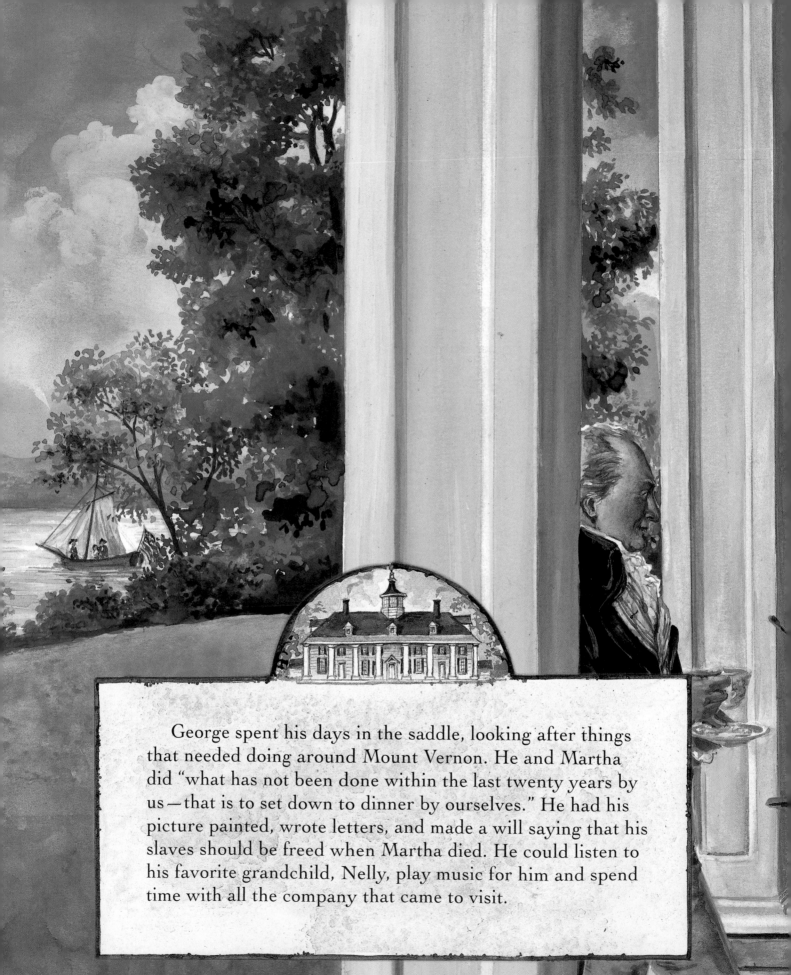

George spent his days in the saddle, looking after things that needed doing around Mount Vernon. He and Martha did "what has not been done within the last twenty years by us—that is to set down to dinner by ourselves." He had his picture painted, wrote letters, and made a will saying that his slaves should be freed when Martha died. He could listen to his favorite grandchild, Nelly, play music for him and spend time with all the company that came to visit.

Not long before his 68th birthday, George went out on his customary ride through the fields of Mount Vernon. By the time he came in from the snowy day, he was chilled and damp, coming down sick. Doctors were sent for, but death finally caught the old fox late in the night of December 14, 1799.

All over the world people mourned for
GEORGE WASHINGTON
"FIRST IN WAR, FIRST IN PEACE,
FIRST IN THE HEARTS OF HIS COUNTRYMEN."

MORE ABOUT GEORGE WASHINGTON

HOW DID HE LOOK? At 6'2" tall, George towered over most men of his day. He was a strong, natural athlete who had "the soul, look, and figure of a hero." He had reddish brown hair pulled back in a pigtail, blue-gray eyes, and terrible teeth. He tried all kinds of false teeth made out of gold and ivory or cows' teeth. They all hurt. George mostly kept his mouth shut.

HIS PARENTS: Augustine Washington, known as Gus, was a tall, sandy-haired man. He and his slaves raised tobacco and ran an ironworks. After his first wife died, he married cantankerous Mary Ball.

HIS BIRTHDAY: According to the style of calendar people had been using since the time of Julius Caesar, Gus and Mary had George on February 11, 1732. When England switched over to the modern calendar, George's birthday became February 22.

HIS FAMILY: George had two older half brothers, Lawrence and Austin, and an older half sister, Jane. Lawrence became George's beloved friend and mentor. George had a younger sister, Betty, and three little brothers, Sam, Jack, and Charles. Gus Washington died when George was 11.

On January 6, 1759, George married a cheerful, dark-haired widow, Martha Dandridge Custis. He called her Patsy. She described herself as an "old-fashioned Virginia house-keeper, steady as a clock, busy as a bee, and cheerful as a cricket." George adopted her little girl and boy, Patsy and Jacky. Later on, George and Martha looked after two grandchildren, Eleanor and George Washington Custis: Nelly and Wash.

EDUCATION: He studied with a tutor and at a log school in Fredericksburg. George wrote out his lessons and 110 *Rules of Civility and Decent Behaviour in Company and Conversation*, such as "Sleep not when others speak" and "Spit not in the fire." After he was 14 or so, he mostly taught himself by reading books.

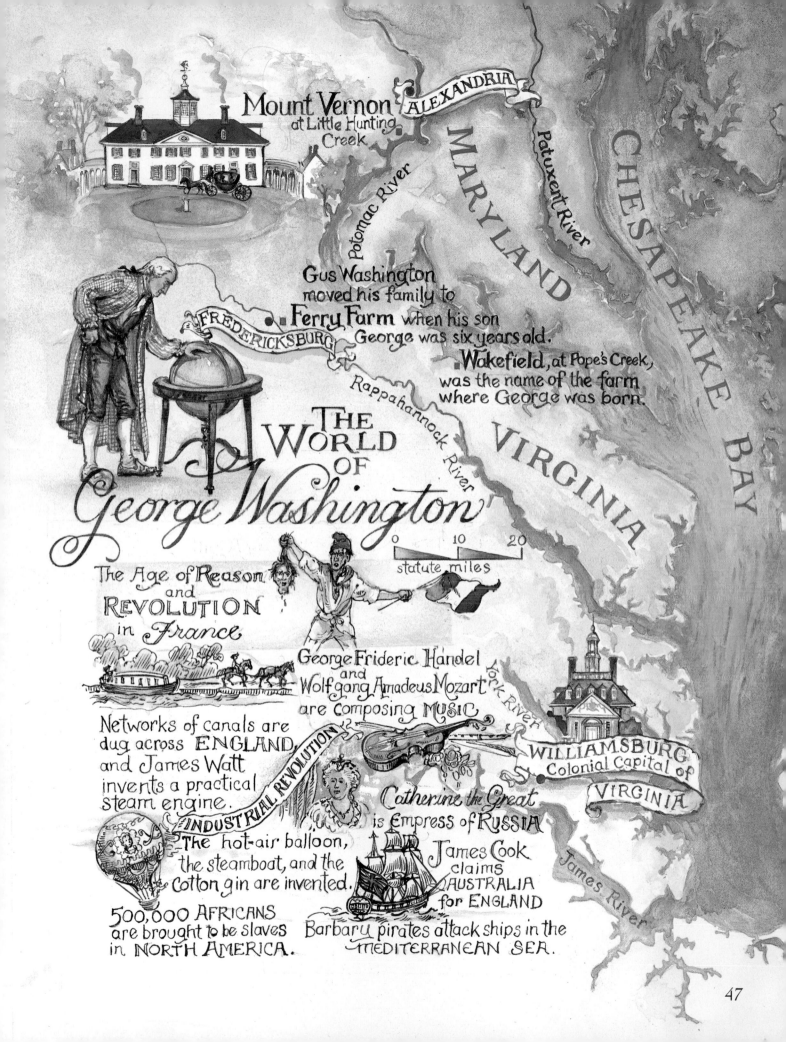

Mount Vernon at Little Hunting Creek

ALEXANDRIA

MARYLAND

Potomac River

Patuxent River

CHESAPEAKE BAY

Gus Washington moved his family to FREDERICKSBURG • Ferry Farm when his son George was six years old.

Wakefield, at Pope's Creek, was the name of the farm where George was born.

Rappahannock River

VIRGINIA

THE WORLD OF George Washington

The Age of Reason and REVOLUTION in France

0   10   20
statute miles

George Frideric Handel and Wolfgang Amadeus Mozart are Composing MUSIC

York River

Networks of canals are dug across ENGLAND, and James Watt invents a practical steam engine.

INDUSTRIAL REVOLUTION

Catherine the Great is Empress of RUSSIA

WILLIAMSBURG Colonial Capital of VIRGINIA

The hot-air balloon, the steamboat, and the cotton gin are invented.

James Cook claims AUSTRALIA for ENGLAND

500,000 AFRICANS are brought to be slaves in NORTH AMERICA.

Barbary pirates attack ships in the MEDITERRANEAN SEA.

James River

For the Founding Mothers, including mine

THE AUTHOR WISHES TO THANK

Willard Sterne Randall for his kind assistance and a swell book; Suzanne Patrick Fonda for her friendship;
Nicholas P. Rosenbach for his genial and astute help with the making of maps; Mary Thompson and the
knowledgeable folks of Mount Vernon, who tell the story of the legendary man of the house; and
George Washington, who sacrificed the pleasure of living there for the sake of his country.

Constitutional Convention 1787

1. George Washington (Va.), 2. James Madison (Va.), 3. Alexander Hamilton (N.Y.), 4. Gouverneur Morris (Pa.), 5. William Jackson, secretary,
6. Rufus King (Mass.), 7. Charles Pinckney (S.C.), 8. John Dickinson (Del.), 9. Richard Bassett (Del.), 10. John Langdon (N.H.), 11. Gunning Bedford, Jr. (Del.);
12. Nathaniel Gorham (Mass.), 13. Hugh Williamson (N.C.), 14. Charles C. Pinckney (S.C.), 15. William Blount (N.C.), 16. Jacob Broom (Del.),
17. Daniel Jenifer (Md.), 18. Richard Dobbs Spaight, Sr. (N.C.), 19. James McHenry (Md.), 20. Nicholas Gilman (N.H.), 21. William Paterson (N.J.),
22. William Few (Ga.), 23. William Livingston (N.J.), 24. Jared Ingersoll (Pa.), 25. John Blair (Va.), 26. George Clymer (Pa.), 27. Jonathan Dayton (N.J.),
28. Daniel Carroll (Md.), 29. David Brearly (N.J.), 30. John Rutledge (S.C.), 31. Pierce Butler (S.C.), 32. Robert Morris (Pa.), 33. Roger Sherman (Conn.),
34. William S. Johnson (Conn.), 35. Thomas Mifflin (Pa.), 36. James Wilson (Pa.), 37. Benjamin Franklin (Pa.), 38. Thomas Fitzsimmons (Pa.),
39. George Read (Del.), and 40. Abraham Baldwin (Ga.). The diagram and key refer to the painting on pages 32–33, which shows 40 of the 55 delegates.

BIBLIOGRAPHY

The American Heritage Book of the Revolution. New York: American Heritage Publishing Company, 1958
Bowen, Catherine Drinker. *Miracle at Philadelphia.* Boston: Little, Brown and Company, 1966
Buckland, Gail and Zweifel, John. *The White House in Miniature.* New York: W.W. Norton and Company, 1994
Jacobs, William Jay. *Washington.* New York: Charles Scribner's Sons, 1991
Randall, Willard Sterne. *George Washington.* New York: Henry Holt, 1997
Seale, William. *The President's House.* Washington, D.C.: White House Historical Association, 1986

Cheryl Harness does her illustrations on Strathmore cold-pressed illustration board, using watercolor, gouache, ink, and colored pencil.

The world's largest nonprofit scientific and educational organization, the National Geographic Society was founded in 1888 "for the increase and
diffusion of geographic knowledge." Since then it has supported scientific exploration and spread information to its more than nine million
members worldwide. The National Geographic Society educates and inspires millions every day through magazines, books, television programs,
videos, maps and atlases, research grants, the National Geography Bee, teacher workshops, and innovative classroom materials. The Society is
supported through membership dues and income from the sale of its educational products. Members receive NATIONAL GEOGRAPHIC magazine—
the Society's official journal—discounts on Society products, and other benefits. For more information about the National Geographic Society
and its educational programs and publications, please call 1-800-NGS-LINE (647-5463) or write to the following address: National Geographic
Society, 1145 17th Street N.W., Washington, D.C. 20036-4688 U.S.A. Visit the Society's Web site: www.nationalgeographic.com

Library of Congress Cataloging-in-Publication Data

Harness, Cheryl.
    George Washington / by Cheryl Harness.
        p.   cm.
    Includes bibliographical references.
    Summary: Presents the life of George Washington,
    focusing on the Revolutionary War years and his presidency.
    ISBN 0-7922-7096-7
    1. Washington, George, 1732–1799 Juvenile literature.
    2. Presidents—United States Biography Juvenile literature.
    3. United States—History—Revolution, 1775–1783 Juvenile literature.
    4. United States—Politics and government—1783–1789 Juvenile literature.
    5. United States—Politics and government—1789–1797 Juvenile literature
    [1. Washington, George, 1732–1799. 2. Presidents.] I. Title.
    E312.66.H28 2000
    973.4'1'092—dc21   99-29920
    [B]

Printed in the United States of America